Wellington, Somerset

Old & New

Postcards and Photographs

by Douglas J. Marshall

Wellington Town lies in the fertile valley of the River Tone (to the north) and the Blackdown Hills (to the south).

On the highest point is the monument to the Duke of Wellington, who took his title from the town in 1812. Unfortunately he did not live here and only visited Wellington once in 1819.

Having been born here and collected postcards and photo's for many years, this is my second illustrated book. More from my collection have been published in other books about the town; all are out of print (see back page).

Douglas Marshall
May 1999

Published by D.J. Marshall
Printed by Maslands Ltd, Tiverton, Devon

Squirrel Hotel, dating back to 1672, had its own Squirrel Bus (horse drawn) to meet the trains and bring customers back up to town for 6d.

Now the home of Wellington Town Council, Museum and Community Offices.

1920c The Squirrel in its hey-day. Large room at rear for dances, wedding receptions, dining room.

FORE STREET, WELLINGTON, SOMERSET.

1929c View to the centre. On the left a drapers shop. Just beyond, the site of Fox's Bank (taken over in 1921 by Lloyds) the last private bank to print £5 notes - there is one in the museum.

FORE STREET, WELLINGTON.

1930c Fore Street. The parking of cars is starting on the road. On the right is the hairdresser's shop of Marshall, where I grew up, the next door garage later became a showroom and offices for Thomas Brickmaker, now the library.

1999 Cars and more cars.

EXPERIMENTAL SHORT WAVE STATION

Q.R.A.
TO RADIO ....

9, FORE STREET
WELLINGTON, SOMERSET, ENGLAND.

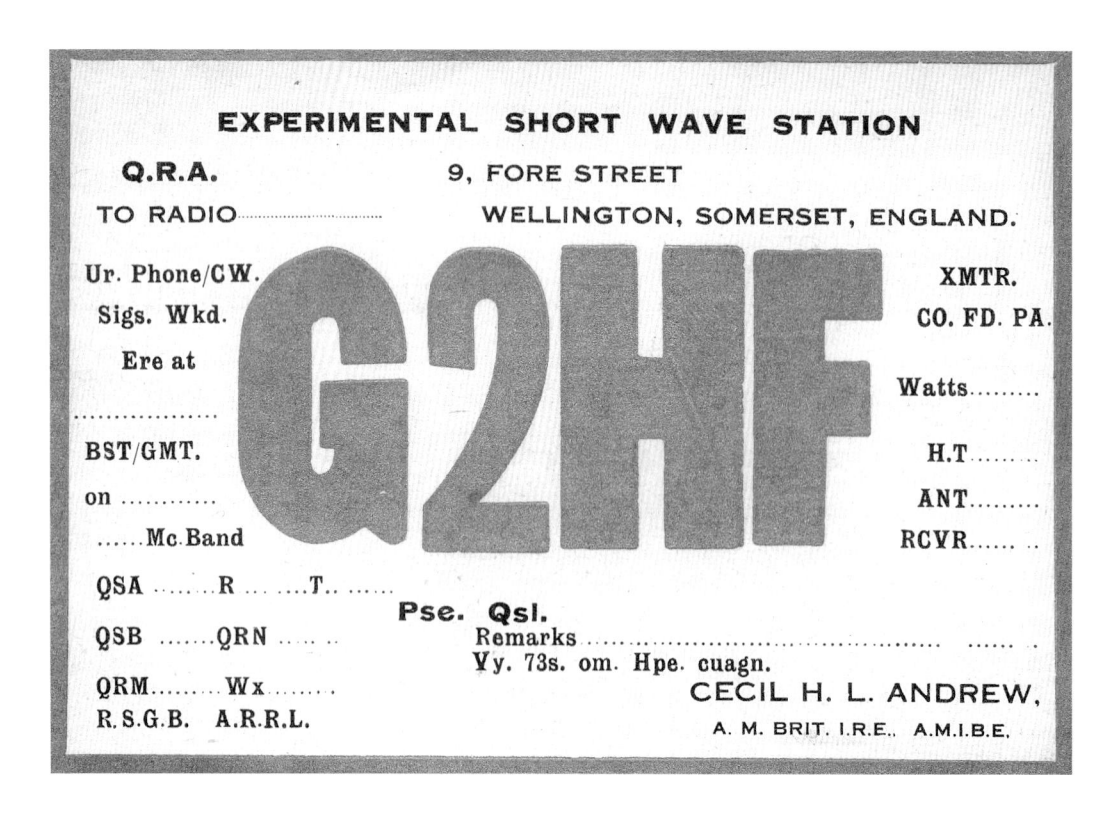

Ur. Phone/CW.
Sigs. Wkd.
Ere at
....
BST/GMT.
on ....
...... Mc. Band
QSA ...... R ...... T ......
QSB ...... QRN ......
QRM ...... Wx ......
R.S.G.B.   A.R.R.L.

G2HF

XMTR.
CO. FD. PA.
Watts ....
H.T ....
ANT ....
RCVR ....

Pse. Qsl.
Remarks ....
Vy. 73s. om. Hpe. cuagn.

CECIL H. L. ANDREW,
A. M. BRIT. I.R.E., A.M.I.B.E.

Cecil Andrews, radio station.

1912c Fore Street. Looking towards the west. Large road with horses and carts, men and women shopping and blinds on the shops to keep the sun off.

1906 An almost empty road in Fore Street looking west. On the left is now the Midland Bank and Somerfield stores.

FIRST MEET OF SIR JOHN AMORY'S STAGHOUNDS
AT WELLINGTON
FEB. 15, 1911

1911 High Street, large crowd to see the hunt.

HIGH STREET, WELLINGTON.

1930c High Street - straight on to Taunton. There are no traffic lights. The clothing and boot shop is now a baker's shop. Beyond the King's Arms was the Baker's Stores grocery (now boots).

1910c High Street. Election fever at the Conservative Club. Has our man won? Toller shop on the left the furniture store is now a tea room.

1999 The Kings Arms passageway now turned into the lounge. The front has been plastered and painted.

1918c The Kings Arms, High Street, Landlord - Tristram in passageway. Cycle Club badge over the doorway.

1999 The club doorway has been moved.

1930c High Street. International Stores. All the staff coming out to have their photo's taken (now a fish and chip shop).

HIGH STREET, WELLINGTON, SOM.

1920c Looking East. Richardson's Garage post in the road - before one car crashed into it!

Gentlemen's Hairdressing Saloon.

Ladies Hairdressing Saloon.

All Sports Goods at Store Prices.

E. T. Hoskins
Hairdresser, Perfumer,
Ornamental Hair Worker
and Tobacconist
High Street, Wellington. Som.

General Saloon.

1925c High Street. Hairdresser's shop showing sports goods and saloon.

19

1912c High Street. Looking towards the centre of town. On the right Mentone House (No. 45) home of the Toms family. The London Inn (small white building) was taken down to make Longforth Road in 1930. On the left is now a furniture store.

WELLINGTON, SOM., ENGLAND.

190

We now supply a very light Folding-Music-Stand, Nickel-Plated, at 5/- Post Free. Polished Brass Stands, 15/-

John R. Toms

TELEGRAMS: "TOMS, WELLINGTON, SOMERSET."

James Kelway Toms, inventor and maker of violin strings. He became deaf at the age of thirty but still made the strings, he died in 1954 leaving over £70,000 - a fortune then.

1953 Queen Elizabeth's Coronation Day street party in Longforth Road, held in Woodbury's coach shed (now site of a petrol station) all clean and cleared out for celebration teas.

1953 Three men dressed as belles for the fancy dress in High Street. Tom Milton, Bill Dunbar and Len Moore.

WELLINGTON.

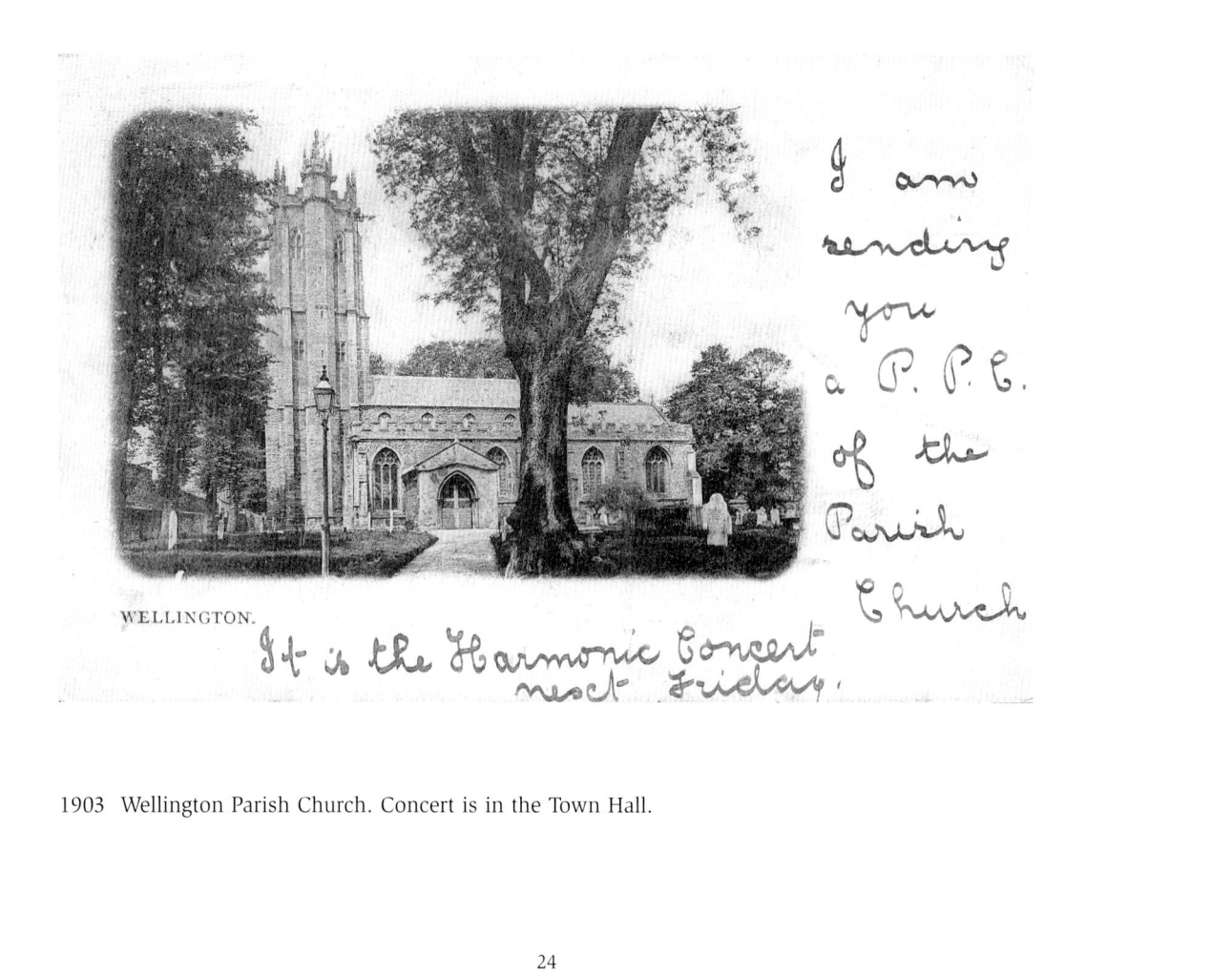

I am sending you a P.P.C. of the Parish Church

It is the Harmonic Concert next Friday.

1903 Wellington Parish Church. Concert is in the Town Hall.

1906 Note the old Wellington coat of arms. Four bags of wool on a blue background with a yellow and white cross

1920c Arthur Street all dressed for a ride to Taunton on his Douglas motor bike. Large warning sign for motorists to drive slowly into Wellington (before traffic lights were installed). Photo taken by Priory House. Arthur played the piano at the Castle Cinema for silent films.

FOX BROS. & CO. LTD.
AERIAL VIEW OF TONEDALE MILLS, WELLINGTON, SOMERSET.

1925c Aerial view of Fox's factory with the railway station and W. Thomas & Co. builders stores and coal yard.

1908 Wellington Station. Steam train with full steam to take it up the gradient towards White Ball tunnel; in 1904 coming down, the City of Truro was clocked at 100 miles per hour.

TONEDALE MILLS, WELLINGTON. SOM.

1920 Fox's showing the main mills. The canteen and the gym have now been taken down and new houses built. The canteen was also used for pantomimes and evacuees were housed there in the Second World War. Dr Ball trained the men in the gym.

1912 The first airman to land a plane in Wellington. Spectators can be seen around the field at Tonedale.

Frenchman Salmet with his Bleriot monoplane. Some 4,000 people came to see it.

Linden House. Sylvanus Fox and his four sisters lived here. One married Edward Burnett Tylor who published a book in 1881 'Introduction to the Study of Man and Civilisation'. He was later made Sir Edward.

High Path, Wellington, Somerset Photo by H. Montague Cooper

This house marked to the right is where I have been

1904 High Path with old Ivy Cottages on the left and a plot of ground on the right waiting to be developed.

1910c Photo taken from the Railway Hotel. In the middle of the road the Squirrel bus on its way back to town with passengers from the Railway Station.

1917 The Athletic Ground, in front of the Grandstand. Wellington Scouts with drums and bugles. The ground, owned by Fox's, was for the use of the people of the town and workers at the mills.

1916c First World War. Flax was grown around the town and a camp set up on the Athletic Ground to house workers who harvested the crop which was used to make canvas for tents and covers for airplanes.

1918c Rag Fair to raise funds for Somerset prisoners of war. Over £1,300 was raised. The Methodist Church can be seen on the skyline.

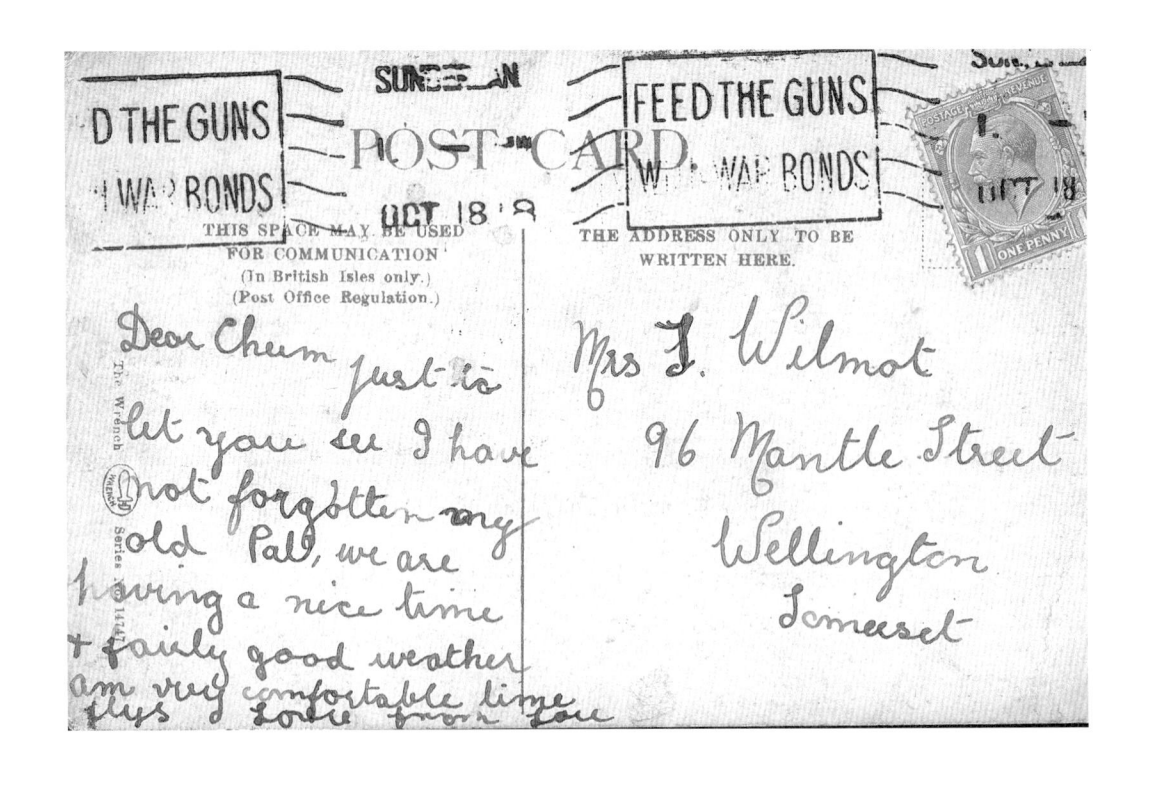

1918 Post card franked 'Feed the guns with war bonds'.

1908 Lifeboat Day. This boat was pulled through the town, taken down to the basins and rides were given to raise funds. How many people can you see on board?

1908 One of four arches around Wellington for the Somerset Agricultural Show held on fields which is now Wellesley Park. Fox's arch can be seen draped with wool.

Waterloo Road, Wellington.

1912 Waterloo Road. Named after the Battle of Waterloo. On the left is the Dolphin Inn, Seymour Street entrance is on the right.

1903 Main entrance from Beech Grove to Wellington Park, given to the town by Fox's. For the opening ceremony on May 2nd, 1903, all shops were closed and there was a procession from the Town Hall to the park. Structural builder was Follett and Bishop Bros. laid water pipes from the Town stream. Morris Veltch of Exeter laid out the park.

1999 The park gates 90-plus years on and still giving pleasure to all. Now, with grants from the National Lottery, we shall see it back to its former glory. The old lamp over the roof - how did they light it?

1906c Open view across the park with the water fountain in full flow.

1908 I wonder who is having their photo' taken on the bridge? The trees are just beginning to grow. The view is towards The Court and Courtland Road.

1940c Courtland Road. Infants in May Day Queen ceremony.

1940c Courtland Road Infants' School head mistress Miss Withers and teacher Miss Windsor who were also Girl Guide leaders (right to left).

1915c The old workhouse in North Street, now site of the Police Station and Lodge Close bungalows and flats. Only the gates and brick piers are standing the building was demolished in 1973.

1925c North Street. A view down towards old cottages pulled down to build the town Fire Station. Behind was the Cattle Market now a car park. Shows some of the shops with blinds to keep out the sun.

1912c North Street. Trickey fruit and veg shop in Coronation dress. This is now a fish and chip shop.

1908c Halfyard & Sons coach builder of North Street with some of his carriages on show. His works and showroom behind later became the Half Moon pub and is now a hairdresser's and offices.

1907c   South Street. On the right is the Town Stream running down the road with metal plates forming bridges for small boys (and girls!) to sail matchbox boats. Shapland's Bakery and Restaurant on the left later moved to Fore Street.

1999 Cars and more cars.

1908   Another arch for the Agricultural Show. The Green Dragon pub on the right. South Street looking towards the centre of town.

1918 South Street. Baptist Church; the iron railings were taken away for the war 1940c to be melted down and recycled.

Garden at Grange Lodge, Blackdown School, The Grange, Wellington, Somerset.

1913 Wellington School. This is the garden of the present Headmaster's home, then used by the Blackdown School, of Wellesley Park, as an infants' school.

1904 Top of South Street the Sanford Arms with the Tuck Shop of Wellington School on its left .

1929 The Wellington School Memorial Chapel for boys of the school who lost their lives in the First World War.

POST CARD.

This space may be used for communication

MEMORIAL CHAPEL.

By far the greater number of our Subscribers have not even seen the Building. We send you therefore this view taken from near the Cottage Hospital on New Year's Day, 1929.

The exterior is now complete, save the Cupola, 26 feet high, which is to be erected in the centre of the roof.

The address only to be written here

Work is now being concentrated on the Interior, the Lighting, Decoration, Seating, Oakwork, and Sanctuary.

We hope before Whitsun to be able to announce the date of the Dedication; this, in all probability, cannot be until October next, much as all would like to see it take place during the Summer Term.

Back of the post card. A large part of the internal work was done by pupils.

1910c The Woodman's Cottage with the game-keeper showing off his catch. The cottage has now gone and the site is overgrown with trees.

1910 Wellington Monument started to be built in 1817 but the money ran out and it took until 1892 to finish in celebration of the Duke of Wellington's victory at Waterloo.

1930c The four cannons around the Monument came from Exeter Quay in 1911. They were then placed on elm carriages. How many people have had their photo's taken sitting on them? This is my father W. Marshall, hairdresser, of Fore Street. The cannons were taken away in the Second World War for scrap.

1985 Unveiling a replacement cannon after a lot of work by Wellington Rotary Club, and help from Exeter City Council who donated the cannon. The carriage was made in Wellington by Rotary in English Oak.

1909c Mr Trenchard of Blue Ball with one of his steam tractors taking a boiler to one of the woollen mills. Mantle Street stores in the background.

1915c Sir John Popham's Almshouses given to the town in 1605c, rebuilt on this site in 1833. Now the home of the Catholic Church.

1980 Wellington Milk Factory, later closed down and demolished. The site is now a housing estate named after the Walker Bros. who started the factory in 1840c.

All Saints Church, Wellington. *I expect you know a little about this building. Eh?*

1905 Rockwell Green Church built in 1889. A tower and spire was added in 1908.

1935 Girl Guides of Rockwell Green showing the cup after winning the district competition. The old school in background.

WESTFORD MILLS, WELLINGTON, FROM THE AIR

1920c Aerial view of Elworthy Woollen Mill at Westford, closed in 1934 with a loss of 200 workers.

A Lucky Pig.

You may push me
You may shuv
But I'm hanged
If I'll be druv
from WELLINGTON.

1916 Postcard sent from Wellington - one of a series of fun cards.

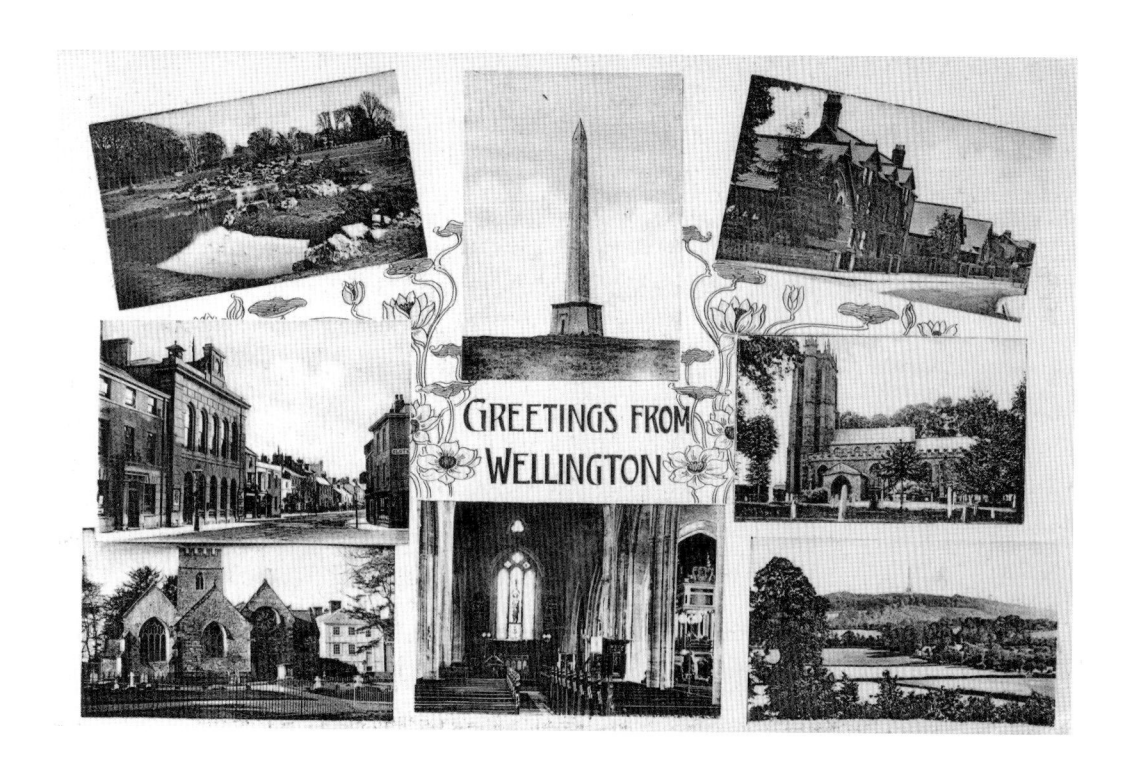

1920 Postcard with eight views around Wellington.

Book of Wellington .... *Allen & Bush 1981*
Wellington in Old Postcards .... *Heal & Marshall 1984*
Yesterday Towns Wellington .... *Allen 1992*

In Wellington Museum may be seen:
Toms Strings, Fox's £5 note, Books of Brickworks, Parish Church, Civil War and many more...

Photographic acknowledgments of postcards:
Frith's series, Parkhouse, Montague Cooper, Surrey Flying Service, Chapman & Son, Fred End, French & Son